Jeremiah Johnson

ISBN-13: 978-31534734388

ISBN-10: 1534734384

This book is lovingly dedicated to our wonderful congregation at Grace Point Church, without your love and support there is no way I could do what I do…

GOD'S NOT A CONTROL FREAK

GOD DOESN'T WANT to control you. He didn't create you to be a robot or a slave. He is not the good-times killer that man-made religion paints him out to be. His plan isn't to come into your life and constantly tell you no. "No, don't do this." "No, don't do that." He is not the author of bondage; he is the author of freedom.

The God that created heaven and earth is not looking to enslave and micromanage his highest creation: mankind, you. He created this big beautiful world for us to enjoy it with him. He wants to give you the freedom to make your own choices and live from your heart.

God is like a loving father that has worked all night to prepare Christmas morning for his children. The tree is decorated and ready, presents are wrapped and under the tree, Christmas cookies are baked and ready to be eaten, everything is prepared. As the children wake up and run screaming into the living room, the father sits back to watch with a big smile on his face. With every squeal of delight and every moment of surprise, the father enjoys his children's excitement. The father isn't looking at the tree; he isn't looking at the presents or the cookies. He is watching his children enjoy what he has prepared for them.

This world was created for you. Beautiful sunrises and sunsets, they were created for you. The happy sounds of birds singing and waves crashing, they were all created for you. The taste of delicious food and the melody of good music, it was created for you. The feeling of falling in love and the joy of your first roller coaster ride, it was created for you. The sight of snowcapped mountains and valleys filled with flowers, they were created for you. The feeling of winning a game or acing a test, it was created for you. The joy of having children and watching them grow up, it was created for you.

From your first breath to your last breath and heaven beyond, it was all created for you to enjoy. God *really* loves you and he wants you to enjoy what he has created for you. All these things are yours and you are his. He enjoys you.

Man-made religion paints a picture of God being one big eternal "NO." I'm here to tell you that he is one big eternal "YES." He has a plan of love and liberty for your life.

1

JESUS'S FIRST SERMON

THERE IS SOMETHING significant about the way we begin something. The first step of a race is always pointed the direction that you are going. The way we start sets the tone and aim of our real purpose. Many times, how we begin reveals the real reason why we came. God makes a very powerful statement in scripture about the way he does things in Isaiah 46:10: "Declaring the end from the beginning, and from ancient times the *things* that are not *yet* done, saying, My counsel shall stand, and I will do all my pleasure."

God declares the end from the beginning. It's his special privilege as creator; he knows exactly how everything ends, even as it begins. He is the Alpha and the Omega, the beginning and the ending; he stands outside of the boundaries of time, so he sees the end of a thing just as clearly as he sees its beginning. I believe it's his joy to kind of sign his name at the beginning of things, giving us a glimpse of how things are going to end up.

This is seen very clearly in the Garden of Eden right after the fall when God says the seed of the woman shall bruise the head of the serpent and the serpent shall bruise his heel. God lays out the entire plan of redemption in that one small statement, declaring the end from the beginning. Jesus, the seed of the woman, crushed the serpent's plans, being bruised himself in the process but bringing an end to his plans. We see God using this method of operating when he preaches the gospel first to Abraham, granting him righteousness by faith and not works.

We can take a look at how Jesus begins his earthly ministry to give us a better idea of what his true mission and goal is.

Let's go to Nazareth, Jesus's hometown, and watch him preach his very first sermon. Jesus is about to kick off and begin his earthly ministry; he has three and a half years to turn the entire world upside down. Let's see the very first step of his race.

Luke 4:16–22:

"So he came to Nazareth, where he had been brought up. And as his custom was, he went into the synagogue on the Sabbath day, and stood up to read. And he was handed the book of the prophet Isaiah. And when he had opened the book, he found the place where it was written:

'The Spirit of the Lord is upon me,

Because he has anointed me

To preach the gospel to the poor;

He has sent me to heal the brokenhearted,

To proclaim liberty to the captives

And recovery of sight to the blind,

To set at liberty those who are oppressed;

To proclaim the acceptable year of the Lord.'

Then he closed the book, and gave it back to the attendant and sat down. And the eyes of all who were in the synagogue were fixed on him. And he began to say to them, 'Today this scripture is fulfilled in your hearing.' So all bore witness to him, and marveled at the gracious words which proceeded out of his mouth. And they said, 'Is this not Joseph's son?'"

He begins with "the Spirit of the Lord is upon me."

Well, what does that mean? It means a lot of things but I want to bring out something about the spirit of the Lord that most folks are less aware of. We see a unique and beautiful truth about the spirit of the Lord in 2 Corinthians 3:17, which says, "Where the Spirit of the Lord is, there is freedom."

Wherever God's spirit is, there in that place will be freedom. God's spirit carries an atmosphere of freedom. Have you ever been in a "dead church" before, where there is an absence of life, an absence of freedom? God, of course, is omnipresent but God might not be dwelling in that place in a manifested presence of his spirit. You see, wherever God's spirit is not there will be the opposite of freedom; there will be bondage, lifelessness, and a distinct absence of liberty. Wherever the spirit of the Lord is there will be *freedom* and the spirit of the Lord was upon Jesus. (We will talk more extensively about this later on in the book.)

If the spirit of the Lord was on Jesus, he was living in freedom and wherever he went freedom went. Jesus came to the towns and cities of Galilee carrying freedom. People came out in droves to see him. They scrambled and pushed together just to touch him. People climbed trees, tore roofs off of houses, and journeyed through crowds just to be near him. The human heart has a cry for freedom. We all want to be free, *because* we were created by God to live in freedom. Just like the birds were created to fly in the skies and fish were created to swim in the sea, we were created to live in freedom.

Jesus carried this atmosphere of freedom; the people wanted to be near him. He was constantly setting people free. Freedom from sickness, freedom from hunger, freedom from pain, freedom from any and all forms of bondage and slavery.

However, not everyone was excited about Jesus and his freedom. The religious people of the day didn't care much for this freewheeling prophet from Nazareth. His freedom challenged them and scared them. They wanted to be feared and they wanted to be in control. This new prophet that walked the shores of Galilee didn't seem to fear anyone or anything. His freedom was attractive to the common people and terrifying for those in control.

Then he goes on to say, "He has anointed me to preach the gospel to the poor." Perhaps one of the greatest forms of slavery is poverty. I grew up poor. My mother was a single momma trying to put herself through college to make a better life for her and her son. I am so grateful for her courage. What she did was not easy and I certainly wasn't an easy child to raise.

During those days, if I heard it once I heard it a thousand times, "Honey, we can't do that; we don't have enough money for that." The lack of finances was very constraining. There is a certain amount of freedom that financial prosperity provides. The Bible says the destruction of the poor is their poverty. Ever wonder why a young woman goes into prostitution or why a young man begins to sell drugs? I know. Not having enough is not fun, and money tries to present itself as a savior and a path to perpetual happiness; it's not.

There are plenty of miserable rich people. The Bible says the love of money is the root of all evil, but money is not evil. It's just a tool; you can help people or hurt people with it. Jesus came bringing freedom for those that don't have enough by supplying their needs. In 2 Corinthians 8:9 it says: "For you know the grace of our Lord Jesus Christ, that though he was rich, yet for your sakes he became poor, that you through his poverty might become rich."

Now, I'm not saying it's God's will for everyone to be filthy rich, but I am saying it is God's will for your needs to be met and for you to have enough to be a joyful giver as well. Any good father provides for his own. Our Father is a good father.

The next thing Jesus says is this: "He has sent me to heal the brokenhearted." I don't know about you, but I've had my heart broken a couple times and there is nothing quite like it: Hurt, rejection, feelings of unworthiness, feelings of not measuring up. The challenge with a broken heart is that many times it doesn't heal up quickly. A broken heart has a hard time believing, a hard time trusting. A broken heart is dominated by fear of it happening again. A broken heart is sore to the touch. When we have something that is sore we generally guard it from being touched so it won't be hurt again. Emotional bondage can be some of the worst kind of bondage.

Jesus has a plan to heal broken hearts and break the cycles of emotional bondage. Not only will he heal us of the past, but he will remove the sting of the emotional pain so we don't have to relive it over and over again. He will then heal our hearts and restore our ability to trust again. He will restore our ability to believe again.

Then Jesus says, "proclaim liberty to the captives." Every person he just mentioned was in bondage in some way. Whether it was financial bondage or emotional bondage, all of these people were having their freedom stolen. Then he goes on to make this broad sweeping statement of freedom. I'm here to "proclaim liberty to the captives!"

The gospel is a declaration of freedom to every man, woman, and child on this earth. Adam put all of humanity into a prison through his disobedience. Jesus has swung wide the prison doors of Adam's disobedience and yelled to all of us, "Come out of darkness into my marvelous light. Come out of fear, come out of shame, come out of pain, come out of sickness, come out of disease, come out of poverty, come out of lack, come out of abuse, come out of being dominated by sin, come out of addictions, come out of depression, come out!"

Jesus goes on to mention "recovery of sight for the blind, to set at liberty those who are oppressed" A lot of times freedom has come but people don't realize it; they are still being oppressed, and they are still being held back. It's one thing to open the prison door but it's another to lift up the heads of the oppressed so they can *see* that the prison door has been opened. So many times bondage is a result of believing lies.

I'm sure many of you have heard the story about how they used to keep circus elephants in control by tying a rope around their legs and tying it too a stake when the elephant is a baby. When the baby elephants would try to get away, the rope and the stake in the ground was just too strong for them. So over time the baby elephant just stopped trying to get free when the rope was tied to its leg. However, we both know a rope tied to a stake in the ground would have no ability to keep a grown elephant captive, but, as long as the elephant believed that it was captive it would stay captive. Its eyes would be closed to its own freedom.

Not only does Jesus want to set us free, but he wants to open our eyes to that freedom so that we will enjoy it.

Jesus says God has sent him "to proclaim the acceptable year of the Lord." God is opening his arms wide with an attitude of acceptance, not rejection. Whosoever will may come! This freedom has been provided for all. Will everyone enjoy this freedom? No, but it has been paid for, for everyone to enjoy. Jesus sets the stage for his earthly ministry with an overwhelming declaration of promised freedom.

Then he concludes his first sermon with this powerful statement of finality: "And he rolled up the scroll and gave it back to the attendant and sat down. And the eyes of all in the synagogue were fixed on him. And he began to say to them, 'Today this scripture has been fulfilled in your hearing.'"

Can you imagine the intensity of this moment? He just rolls up the scroll and sits down, everybody there staring at him. Can you imagine the power that filled up that room, as the one who actually prophesied through Isaiah 700 years before has come to earth to finally fulfill his promise of freedom? At this time in Jesus's ministry hardly anyone knows him, but they are about to know him; he is about to set the world on fire with freedom. He is going to break every chain and set the captives free. In this little synagogue in Nazareth God declares the end of Jesus's ministry from the beginning. The cross, the place of greatest bondage and slavery, would give birth to a freedom so powerful it would shake the very foundations of hell, death, and the grave.

2

BORN TO BE WILD

MY PARENTS WERE divorced when I was five years old and my mother decided to move back to her hometown, London, Kentucky. We moved in with my grandmother while my mom got back on her feet. My father stayed back in Tonga and never paid any child support, meaning all of the financial responsibility fell onto my mother's shoulders. She spent some time working in different places trying to make ends meet, but ultimately she realized if she was going to provide a better life for us as a family she would have to go back to college.

The summer after my third-grade year my mother and I moved to Richmond, Kentucky. She would begin school the next semester, courageously looking to provide a better life for her and her son. Of course, initially

I was really nervous about changing schools and starting a new life, but at the same time I was excited.

My mother worked a part-time job and went to school full time. She was making sacrifices now that would provide a better future for us. She was very, very busy, which gave me a lot of freedom and a lot of free time.

Eastern Kentucky's college campus presented a whole new world for me; it was like an entirely different planet compared to the small town I had just moved from. We lived in the family housing on the college campus, which consisted of rows and rows of apartments, duplexes, and trailers. There were many families going back to school and plenty of families means plenty of kids.

There were kids everywhere, and I jumped into this new social framework of college campus kids. There was a main street that ran through the community called Brockton. The local elementary school had a name for us: "Brockton kids." It wasn't an affectionate term. All of our parents were busy with school and work, trying to provide a better life for their families. We all probably didn't have as much supervision as we should have. We were a little unruly, to say the least.

In many ways during that time the world was a

different place. We could just jump on our bikes on a hot summer day and roam the campus as long as we were home for dinner that night. There was a public pool at the college and an arcade with pool tables and bowling lanes. The football stadium was the perfect place to ride a skateboard, with all its ramps and hills. In some ways it was preteen paradise.

During that time MTV wasn't just a channel that constantly showed reality TV shows. For us, in the late 80s and early 90s, MTV embodied all that was cool: rock stars and rappers wearing all the latest fashions, living in millionaire mansions, driving Ferraris filled with beautiful girls, they preached to us their messages of partying and freedom. We were diligent students as we sat in from of the TV studying what was cool and what was not, just waiting to see what MTV would say next.

The five-minute music videos that played 24/7 appeared to create a world of absolute fun and freedom with no negative consequences in sight. It was attractive, it was exciting, and we all wanted to be those stars and live their lives. Combine this with the blockbuster movies filled with Rambos and Jean Claude Van Dammes and all manner of action heroes living lives of freedom, liberty, and no consequence. The world began to paint broad strokes of freedom on its big billboard:

"Follow me and all your dreams will come true. I promise you a life filled with freedom and good times."

During this time, I can remember Christians at school that would try to witness to me, speaking to me about sin, hell, and judgment. Initially it scared me a little and caused me to think, but, as I watched their lives, there was nothing at all attractive about it. They seemed to be miserable and it just looked to me like they just had extra rules that no one else had. When I weighed the lifestyle of freedom that MTV and Hollywood promised me against their promises of misery on earth and a shot at eternal life, my young heart easily chose the path that looked like freedom.

All these exciting images of free-for-all parties, no one telling us what do, and good times that would never end were really all just lies. I couldn't see past the images on the screen into the real lives of these superstars whose lives were actually falling apart all around them. I could only see the promise of freedom and fun with no consequences.

Second Peter 2:19 says, "While they promise them freedom, they themselves are slaves of corruption; for by whom a person is overcome, by him also he is brought into bondage."

The world promises freedom but it's not a real

freedom; it ultimately leads us into bondage. True freedom had approached me in school through the Christians who were trying to witness to me, but their freedom was masked with the chains of man-made religion. *They* weren't even enjoying their own freedom; how could they display it and invite me into it? They couldn't: they were bound and the beautiful Jesus that was within them couldn't be seen. The author of liberty was in them but he wasn't having full expression. So, instead of embracing Jesus, who is true freedom, I settled for a well-manufactured lie that promised freedom but delivered slavery.

Initially sin seems like freedom. You think, "Hey I can do whatever I want and no one can tell me what to do!" On the surface that can look, sound, and even feel like freedom, but that type of freedom only lasts for a short while. See, there is something very interesting about sin that most Christians don't generally talk about. Hebrews 11:25 describes Moses as "Choosing rather to suffer affliction with the people of God, than to enjoy the pleasures of sin for a season."

The Bible doesn't say sin isn't pleasurable; it makes it clear that it will only be pleasurable for a season. The pleasure of sin is not lasting and the freedom it promises is very short lived. In the days ahead on that college campus, as my innocence was waylaid and destroyed, initially it was fun; initially it felt like freedom, but what I didn't know was that chains were secretly forming around me and what looked like promised freedom became the trapdoor to slavery.

3

POTS AND PANS

THAT FIRST YEAR on Eastern's college campus was filled with lessons. I was thrust into that unique vibrant social system of many kids with too much freedom and busy exhausted parents trying to make a better future for their families.

Although I began hesitant and intimidated, by year two I was in full stride. Going into the fifth grade I was an early bloomer, I was tall and looked much older than I actually was. The stage was set for opportunity. Over the summer of fourth grade I discovered something that would change my life forever. *I could fix my hair*. Now, remember, this was the late 80s. The 80s are known for many things and one of those things was big hair. I found out that the girls liked long hair and I could grow it out by the truckload. Armed with a can of hair spray, a brush, and my newly acquired skill of "teasing hair," I set out to grow a frock of blonde hair so mantastic that Bret Michaels would be envious. (And, no, there will be no pictures in this book; there are some things that cannot be unseen once seen.)

As I began my pursuit of 80s glam rock hair, I started to get the attention of some of the older girls. With my long lean frame, ripped jeans, and Bret Michaels hair, I looked like I was 16 or 17 years old even though I was still in grade school. The whole time pursuing the world's invitation of fun and freedom, I was trying to turn my life into a rock video; after all, I just wanted to have fun, be free and do whatever I wanted, whenever I wanted to do it.

I caught the attention of a beautiful, unusually confident, blonde-haired, blue-eyed girl named Jennifer. She was sixteen at the time and all the high school guys wanted her but for some strange reason she wanted me. She was very bold and made her intentions very clear. I was flattered but very intimidated. This girl was in high school and I was just a snotty-nosed grade-school kid that had just learned how to fix his hair. She didn't care how old I was; she wanted to date me. I was starstruck and head over heels in puppy love. My hand gripped tighter around my can of hairspray. My ripped jeans and big blonde hair was gonna make me a school bus stop star. Before I knew it I was singing "Every rose has its thorn" to Jennifer every night on the phone.

That year, it was all I could do to keep from getting beat up by all the high school guys because they were so jealous. I had all this freedom and I was growing up way too fast. However, I didn't know it, but chains were preparing and forming around me, and I had no idea. I was just having the time of my life as my innocence evaporated.

This was before texting or Snapchat so we communicated the old-school way, through passing notes. Every day there were notes passed at the bus stop. One day Jennifer passed me a note that would change my life forever. She was going to steal some pot (marijuana) from her aunt and we were going to smoke it together. Up to this point, even in the midst of all the music videos I watched promising a life of freedom, I never really wanted to drink or do drugs. I knew all the rock stars did it but it just wasn't something I was interested in. However, I *was* interested in Jennifer and this was what she wanted. We began to pass notes about it, and, instead of writing marijuana or pot, we had a code phrase: we called it pots and pans. She talked about when she would get the pots and pans from her aunt so we would could have a good time.

The day finally came and we smoked together, and,

like sin manages to do, for a short while, it seemed like freedom and it was fun. As is the nature of all sin, it can never stay contained, it will always demand more and more room in our lives. I started drinking and experimenting with other drugs. Eventually Jennifer dropped the "let's just be friends" note and broke my heart, but the seeds of addiction had been planted and the chains of my sin continued to tighten around me.

4

BIG BOX OF FIREWORKS

FOLLOWING MY RELATIONSHIP with Jennifer, I continued to spend time with the older kids in the neighborhood and experimenting with drugs and alcohol. Things became worse and worse and more out of control. I was developing quite a name for myself and I enjoyed the infamy. Even though the chains around me were forming, they were still invisible and I didn't notice them yet.

We began to dip our hands into all sorts of vandalism, from setting off smoke bombs in the dormitory elevators to throwing parties in the empty trailers in the campus housing area. At times we felt invincible; we lacked any self-control. I was getting into a lot of trouble and I was driving my mother crazy; this whole time, she was just trying to finish school and move on with a better life.

It all came down to a guy named Dustin and a box of fireworks. It was the summer of my sixth-grade year and his family was out of town for the weekend. My friends and I knew he had a big box of fireworks in his house because he had been bragging about it for weeks. We decided we would break into his house and steal them.

We rode our bikes and our skateboards down to his house. At this point the campus police knew me by name and I knew we would have to be very careful not to get caught. It had come to the point that if they even saw me they would get suspicious. This freedom I was pursuing had a high cost.

A Hawaiian guy named Kanoa and myself went around back to see if any of the windows were unlocked. The kitchen window above the sink was unlocked; I hoisted Kanoa up and he crawled through the window and then let me in the back door. We searched the house and found the big box of fireworks in Dustin's parents' closet. We grabbed them and a handful of change to get us all into the campus pool later. We hopped on our bikes and rode to one of the abandoned trailers to stash the fireworks so we could use them later. We were all laughing and giddy with nervousness. We felt invincible. We felt free.

We took the change that we stole and rode our

bikes to the campus pool. We all went swimming and spent time discussing our plans to wreak havoc on the campus dormitories with our newly acquired fireworks later that night. Kanoa came up to me with a big smile on his face and pulled a checkbook at of his backpack and said, "Hey, you wanna make some money?" Earlier, as we were rummaging through the house looking for fireworks he had found a checkbook but didn't say anything to the other guys about it. Initially I was mad at him but, as is the nature of sin, it's really hard to contain and control. Sin always says, "A little further—you've come this far, you might as well go a little farther, just a little."

With excitement in his eyes he explained to me that all we had to do was write a check to ourselves and cash it at the local bank right off campus. He was older than me and had his own paper route and really was quite industrious for a teenager when it came to money. He was confident that we wouldn't get caught and all I could think about was having a pocket full of free money. At that time money meant endless video games, big plates full of breadsticks at the campus grill, bags of candy at the university store, as much pool time as we wanted; money looked and sounded like freedom.

After much daydreaming and deliberation, we wrote the check for $150 and hopped on our bikes to go and commit our first felony. At the time we were not thinking about felonies or burglary charges; all we could think about was the freedom this money was going to give us.

Because of Kanoa's paper route he went to this bank often. We didn't even go inside; we rode up to the drive-through window on our bikes. I was scared to death. My heart was thumping in my chest. I didn't know what to do, other than just stand there and try not to look nervous.

Kanoa greeted the teller, stuffed the check into the tube, and sent it over to her. We stood there in intense silence; it seemed like an eternity went by. I thought to myself this is never gonna work. I was just waiting for the SWAT team to come bursting out of the bushes to arrest us. Then, all of a sudden I hear the sound of the tube coming back down. With a smile on her face the teller thanked us and told us to have a good day. I couldn't believe it. We grabbed the envelope, hopped on our bikes and rode down the road.

Once we thought we were at a safe distance, we pulled the envelope out. Sure enough, $150 cash: we looked at each other with joy and disbelief, jumping up and down. We split it right down the middle. I took $75 dollars and shoved it into my pocket. Wow! It felt good! I felt powerful! I felt free!

However, as is the case with all sin, it doesn't respect its borders and it doesn't stay contained long. As we both discussed what to do with our share of the money, slowly we decided that $75 dollars wasn't enough; we both needed to have $150 and, after all, it was so easy to do the first time we might as well do it again, just one more time, just a little further. So we rode back down to the bank and did the exact same thing. What we didn't know was the second time we came the teller called the police. We split the second envelope of money hopped on our bikes and decided to go our separate ways.

My life was about to change forever.

As I rode off into that beautiful summer day, I felt like I was in a movie or a music video. My freedom was at an all-time high. As I daydreamed about all the possibilities. I heard a very familiar and scary sound behind me, squeaking brakes. I'm not sure why, but all the campus police cars sounded exactly the same when they stopped; my heart leaped into my throat as I turned around to hear, "Young man, may I have a word with you?" My "freedom" came crashing down as he put me into the police cruiser and took me down to the station. What I didn't know was that they had already picked up Kanoa and were questioning him in a different room. We both cracked like the scared kids that we were, and before I knew it my mother was at the police station, furious.

The consequences were heavy and they didn't feel like freedom. The family pressed charges against us. We were charged with second degree burglary and two counts of forgery. Both counts of forgery were felonies all by themselves; these were serious charges. Kanoa got off easier than me because, up until this point, he hadn't been in trouble on the campus. The campus police knew me by name. The campus police met with my mother to express that they had dealt with too much concerning me. They were going to kick us off campus; they said she could continue to go to school there, but we couldn't live on campus any longer.

Leaving campus was a huge blow to us financially. My mother was devastated, I was devastated, and nothing about this felt like freedom. We had to move into the roughest part of Richmond; it was all that we could afford. I had to change schools and leave all my friends behind. I went to juvenile court and I was prosecuted, getting two years of probation, and I was grounded for an undetermined amount of time.

I can remember after we had moved everything into our tiny little apartment in the ghetto of Richmond, Kentucky, and the shock of everything had started to die down. I stood in the apartment doorway and looked out onto the streets. I hadn't given up on this freedom yet; I would have the good times that the TV and the movies promised me. I hadn't yet realized that the freedom I was pursuing was a lie. Like a bull doomed to death I charged ahead to chase the red cape of liberty as the devil masterfully led me into more slavery.

5

INNOCENCE GONE

I CONTINUED TO BELIEVE in this elusive worldly freedom, but as I pursued it the price tag kept getting higher and higher. By the time I got out of high school, I was a full-blown drug addict and alcoholic. The false freedom I had been pursuing proved to be a flat-out lie, but it was now too late—I was trapped. The once invisible chains that the enemy had started forming in my youth were quite visible now. They were visible to everyone. The few short years after high school were an absolute downward spiral of partying and addiction. I lost two of my best friends to drug overdoses. One died of a cocaine overdose, the other of a methadone overdose. The sweet song of freedom was turning into a funeral march.

I can remember once I got several grams of cocaine to do by myself, alone in my room; I thought I was going to die. I couldn't undo the drugs; they were already in my system. All I could do was just lay sweating in my bed, my heart feeling like it was going to explode out of my chest. I lay there staring at the ceiling, half hoping I wouldn't die, half hoping I would; death seemed like the only way out. I couldn't quit. No matter who I hurt, no matter what it cost, my life was being destroyed by these chains but there seemed to be no way out. There was a hollowness to my eyes and a hopelessness to my steps. I felt trapped. I was no longer in control of my own life.

At this point I really wanted to quit and every day was my "last day." I had tricked myself into always believing that I was going to quit tomorrow. The drugs became my master; they told me what I could and couldn't do. The once bright-eyed boy with a heart for adventure was gone. My eyes were dull and hopeless and my heart was crushed by these heavy chains. I could see no way out.

Addiction became my master. I couldn't do anything without getting high or drunk first. Getting high became my number one priority, the first thing I thought of when I got up in the morning and the last thing I thought of when I went to bed at night. Getting high consumed me; it consumed my thoughts, it consumed my time, it was consuming my life. All my relationships began to fall apart, because no one could trust me.

Addiction turns us into something that God never created us to be. We do things we would never normally do and say things we would never normally say, and generally the people we hurt the most are the people that love us the most because they are willing to put up with us the longest. No one could trust me. I couldn't even really trust myself. I was no longer in control, I was enslaved to something that had promised me freedom. Second Peter 2:19 states, "While they promise them freedom, they themselves are slaves of corruption; for by whom a person is overcome, by him also he is brought into bondage."

I had been promised freedom through all the well-devised lies of popular culture, the music, the movies, the TV programs and magazines. If I had just been wise enough to pay attention to the lives of those people, I would have realized that none of them were truly happy, none of them were truly free. I once read a quote in *Rolling Stone* magazine from a very famous rock star, very rich, and well respected by his peers. He said, "You don't know what true misery is like until you have everything you have ever wanted and you're still miserable." Pretty insightful statement. I think King Solomon pretty much came to the same conclusion.

What I needed was a hero to break the chains off of my life; I had lost control and I needed something greater and stronger than me to set me free. I never in a million years dreamed this freedom that I had been desperately searching for was Jesus. Nobody seemed less free than the Christians I had seen, but I was getting desperate and my options were running out.

6

FREEDOM BLOOMS

Y MOTHER HAD some experiences growing up that really turned her off to the church. Because of her experiences with just good people serving God the best way they knew how but laboring under the yoke of condemnation and man-made religion, she chose to stay as far away from organized religion as possible. However, during my rebellion, she reached a point in her life where her heart began to yearn for something more. She began to search for some sort of spirituality. I don't think she had any intention of it being Jesus, but Jesus is really good at changing our plans.

During that season of her life there was a lady at her work that she really didn't know personally but had seen often. One day this lady approached her and said, "I keep seeing your face when I pray. Would it be OK if

I prayed with you?" My mother was so taken by surprise she really didn't have a chance to refuse. This lady took my mother by the hand and led her into the women's restroom and prayed for her. When my mother later told me about all this she said, "I felt something like a tornado go through my body and then I felt peace." My mother had never actually "felt" God before; she was amazed and excited. She started going to church with this lady and loved it.

At this time, I was at one of the lowest points of my life. I was in a lot of trouble with the police and had several warrants out for my arrest. I had written several thousand dollars' worth of bad checks to get drugs. (I didn't actually write the checks to the drug dealers. Drug dealers don't take checks from drug addicts; they are smarter than that.) I wrote the checks to local supermarkets and businesses that would allow me to buy something and then write the check for over the amount of the item and get cash back. My days would consist of getting up driving to a grocery store, getting a case of beer, writing the check for as much over the amount as they would allow me, getting cash back and then going to the drug dealer's house and picking up drugs, then spending the rest of my day riding around drinking and getting high.

I was really depressed and I knew I was going to get

caught any day and go to jail but I had completely lost all control of my life. The addictions and depression had turned me into the walking dead.

I had been doing this for several months and the bad checks were piling up. Each check written was a felony. I was in a really bad place; I just didn't care anymore about anything. My mom started inviting me to church; she seemed happier and was living life with a new sense of purpose. I decided to go with her to a Tuesday night midweek service. This was not because I thought I was going to get anything out of it but because honestly I just wanted to get her off my back.

I remember when I first walked into the foyer of the church; immediately, I could tell something was different. There was something in the air, a presence. Looking back on it I realize now it was the presence of God. Little did I know I would spend the next fourteen years of my life in this church and be there virtually every time the doors were open. I actually encountered God there; it was exciting.

This church was alive with God's presence. The pastor immediately realized I had a call of God on my life and he took me under his wing and began to mentor me. I got a very hard job in a local factory and I began to work, go to church, and pay back all my debts. For the first time in a long time I had structure and purpose in my life. I fell in love with Jesus and realized that he loved me and had created me to enjoy life with him. I began to taste *real* freedom. My relationship with God was exciting. I began to have encounters with his presence. Those first few years were amazing. I had finally found the freedom that I had been searching for. I began to realize that freedom wasn't a party, or a drug, or a girl, or a pocket full of money. Freedom wasn't what I saw play out on the movie or television screen. Freedom was a person and his name was Jesus.

I was genuinely in church every time the doors were open. I began to pray and study my Bible and get to know this God that saved me. Over time the chains of addiction began to drop off of my life. It was a slow process, first the hard drugs, then the alcoholism, and finally marijuana. I was no longer in bondage to any form of substance. It did not have control over myself any longer. This freedom felt amazing.

I had always had a deep sense of fear every time I saw a police officer (usually because I was doing something wrong) but now when I saw a police officer on the road I no longer tensed up and got nervous. I wasn't afraid of death anymore because I knew heaven would ultimately be my home. I was no longer afraid of failure because my life was on the right track and God and I were going places together. I had never known a freedom like this before. It was amazing. I eventually married my high school sweetheart in that church. She had stuck with me through thick and thin, and finally things were looking good.

As I enjoyed this newfound freedom, I began to discover that God had placed gifts inside of me. I told everyone about this freedom that I had found in Jesus. I began to preach and teach. I learned how to play an instrument and joined the praise and worship team at church. I eventually joined a Christian rock band that traveled and did outreach out of the church. I became a youth pastor and ran the teen center in the downtown area of our city. Then I became the associate pastor in a church plant that we did in a neighboring city. Promotion after promotion, open door after open door.

I kind of felt like the apostle Paul when he said in Galatians 1:14: "And I advanced in Judaism beyond many of my contemporaries in my own nation, being more exceedingly zealous for the traditions of my fathers."

Of course I wasn't in Judaism but I was on the fast track to success in ministry. I was the golden child. I was the one parents would refer to when they talked to their kids about someone being "on fire for God."

What I didn't know was that in the midst of all

the wonderful things that were going on, there was a different set of chains the enemy was slowly forming around me, a different type of bondage, a different type of slavery—one that was subtler, more intoxicating and harder to notice than the worldly chains of addiction and alcoholism that I had been set free from. These chains started out invisible and went undetected for many years, but slowly and methodically my freedom was once again being taken away from me. In many ways these chains were worse and more deceiving than the worldly chains I had just been set free from. Outwardly these chains looked good but inwardly they were full of dead men's bones. The chains of man-made religion were forming and when they were done I would be going under the greatest yoke of slavery I had ever known.

7

THE BOILING POT

NOW, AS I write the next portion of this book, I do not in any way want to defame, accuse, or scandalize anyone. The Bible makes it very clear that we do not war against flesh and blood. I do not count myself to be the enemy of any single person or organization on earth. I am called to love people and set the captives free with the truth of the good news. I do, however, have an enemy and I'm fighting him now as I write this book.

A beautiful by-product of declaring truth is exposing Satan's lies. In this chapter, I'm going to share some of my experiences that were very negative in the church that I was mentored in. The Bible says that we are epistles, we are letters that are read by people; our lives are testimonies of the greatness of God. What I'm about to share is a part of my story. We *all* have a story to tell and the intention is that we can help each other along the way.

This part of my testimony is just as important as the drug addiction and alcoholism that I already shared. The devil hates our freedom and he tries to steal it every chance he gets in any way he can trick us into giving it up.

I travel and preach in many different places, meeting all kinds of people, and I have realized that I am not alone in what I'm about to share with you. Unfortunately, the story I'm about to tell is all too common. The names and places change but it's the same stupid attack from the same stupid enemy. The devil has no new tricks. I will stop and say it again: my goal here is not to slander any person or any organization. I do believe people and organizations can recover from this trap, but it does take humility and admitting that the direction you were going in was wrong.

What I'm about to share is very personal and I wouldn't share it at all if I didn't think it was going to help people. It's important for people to speak out when there has been abuse. If we hide it and don't say anything about it, we just set up the next generation to go through the same things we did. We must expose the lies of the enemy, not only for the coming generations but for the people who have gone through these things but feel all alone. There is so much in healing in finding out you are not alone. You are not crazy and other people have gone through the same things. There is life after abuse but we have to rise up and pull back the curtain and reveal the ugliness of spiritual abuse in order to dismiss the shame and allow people to move on with their lives.

Let's declare truth, expose lies, and recognize that those that hurt us were just as much victims as we were. The devil does not play nice and he does not play fair; he hurts everyone involved. He hates our freedom and he seeks to destroy it at all costs.

So my story of man-made religious bondage begins…

The first years at the church I started going to were awesome, but, over time, slowly things began to change. What immediately comes to my mind is an old analogy of boiling a frog in hot water. It goes like this: if you put a frog in a pot of boiling water he will immediately jump out, but if you put him in cold water and then slowly increase the heat the frog won't recognize the danger and end up cooked. I know this may be a bit of a gruesome analogy (we do eat frog legs in the South, and, yes, it does taste like chicken). This analogy does, however, give us an accurate picture of one of the ways the devil operates.

Each time we see the enemy approaching someone in the Bible to deceive them, we see him mixing a little bit of truth with a little bit of lies. He did it went he tempted Adam and Eve in the garden; he did it when he tried to tempt Jesus in the desert. He is sneaky and subtle with his lies. Many times he won't give a bold-faced lie for us to swallow hook, line, and sinker; he will sprinkle it with truth to make it look attractive, then hook us with the deception. I don't say these things to glorify him or to suggest that we should fear him, but Paul says in 2 Corinthians 2:11 that he forgives them "To keep Satan from getting the advantage over us; for we are not ignorant of his wiles and intentions."

There is wisdom in being aware of how he operates so we can shut him down in the future and stop him from operating in any area of our lives.

All that being said, I loved that church and that pastor and I am eternally grateful for everything that I learned there. I made some of the closest friends I have ever had in my life at that place, which makes what the devil managed to accomplish so much more evil. It started very subtly. Slowly the pastor started preaching less and less about Jesus and more and more about himself. The focus started to gradually shift from the goodness of God to the goodness of our pastor.

Jesus wasn't the star of the show anymore; the spotlight steadily turned from shining on the cross and began to shine only on the pastor. The sermons began to be filled with the pastor's accomplishments and how awesome his faith was, how much he had given, how much he had prayed, how much he had told people about Jesus, and what he had to give up to bring him to the place he was now. Slowly, like a pot beginning to boil, our church became a place where we worshipped our pastor and not God.

It wasn't something that was said publicly, flat out, "Hey, we're here today to worship Pastor So-and-So because he is so awesome!" It wasn't like that but gradually the focus of the entire ministry was changing from what Jesus had done to what our pastor had done.

As the pastor began to be lifted up into this exalted place, a blanket of control was spread out over the people. We began to believe that the pastor could hear God for us better than we could hear God for ourselves. Slowly his opinion of us became, in our minds, like God's approval of us. It gave us a sense that if the pastor was displeased with us, that meant that God was displeased with us. This attitude gave him tremendous control over our lives. We didn't want to disappoint

God; I mean, he is the one that saved us. Since we were taught that our pastor was closer to God than we were, we began to live our lives to please the pastor and the other leadership of the organization.

I know that this sounds completely crazy to anyone who has never experienced anything like this before, but to those of you that have I'm sure these words ring chillingly true. Every single area of our lives came under the control of the church, from our finances to the way we raised our children, our marriages, and even what happened in our bedrooms.

We were so afraid of our pastor and displeasing him in any way, we came under his control. We began to put him and the church before everything else in our lives. Our marriages, our children, our jobs, our families all came to be a very distant second to him and the church.

You can imagine the impact it had; it was very destructive. I watched marriages crumble and fall to pieces as people put the pastor and the church before their spouses. I watched children raised in that type of atmosphere resentfully walk away from their parents and ultimately from the Lord because they were put in last place over and over again. I watched people fall into financial ruin as they gave all of their money to the pastor and the church. I watched single mothers give their last dollar and be unable to buy diapers for their babies or food for their children.

It was truly sad, and those of you who have never experienced anything like this before are probably thinking, why in the world wouldn't you just walk away from that craziness? We were like the frog in the pot of water: what began as something so beautiful and so totally about Jesus had become a pit of self-righteous religious destruction. You see, the enemy is quite subtle with his attack. The Bible very clearly says that God should come first in our lives; that is true and healthy, but the way it's presented many times is off.

You see, the pastor is not God. The church is not God. Are pastors good? Absolutely. It's wonderful and biblical to have a pastor. I am a pastor for goodness' sake; I am for them, not against them. Are churches good? Absolutely. It is such a blessing to have a place to gather where we know we are loved and we know we are going to encounter Jesus through his body. The Bible encourages us to come together and warns us against forsaking the assembly of ourselves. So pastors are great and churches are great, but, once again, they are not God.

Having God as first place in our lives is not synonymous with having our church or our pastor as first place in our lives, and if we think it is, things can get really messed up.

Putting God first in our lives is first and foremost receiving from him, not serving him. remember Martha and Mary? Martha put serving the Lord above receiving from him. Mary chose that which was needful; she sat at Jesus's feet and received from him first. Jesus reproved Martha but honored Mary.

When we think our relationship with God is based primarily on serving him rather than receiving from him, we develop a condition called "older brotherism." We labor hard in the field but never get to *know* the father's heart. It's a sad disease and it will leave you accusing folks and being offended at your father's kindness and mercy, and what's worse is you won't *know* him, just work for him.

The primary dynamic of our relationship with God is first and foremost receiving from him. Now, I'm not saying we shouldn't serve him (I'm serving him by writing this book); serving him is important but it takes a distant backseat to knowing him. If I think the primary focus of my relationship with God is serving him, then I can begin to look at church like it is God rather than God being God.

The control was getting stronger and stronger. We

lived in fear of disappointing the pastor; everything we did, everything we said, all revolved around pleasing him and the other leadership of the church because we thought that's what we did to please God.

Also, at this time the sermons began to be more and more about money and how we should give more. The pressure to give became extremely intense. People were basically shamed if they didn't give. Eventually almost everything that was preached about was money and how we should give more. Sermons began to look more like verbal beat downs about how we weren't giving enough, we weren't praying enough, we weren't reading our Bibles enough, how we didn't have enough faith, and the whole time the pastor was set up to be the pinnacle of all spirituality.

If we could just be more like him and his wife, then we would be blessed. The focus of the entire church was now about them and the ministry that we were in. The focus was no longer on Jesus, and when Jesus is the not the focus you can bet it's just a matter of time until all freedom goes out the window.

This church that once operated in so much freedom and liberty was turning into a very spiritually abusive relationship.

I knew many people in the church who couldn't

pay their bills or get diapers for their kids because they were being pressured to give so much. Some people were kicked out of their homes because they were not able to pay their rent. Others ran out of gas and had their electricity shut off. I could tell you story after story of people doing without. It was really sad and it is kind of hard to really convey in words the fullness of what was going on.

Toward the end of my time at that church I was more in bondage than when I first walked through the doors. Heavy chains of man pleasing legalism drug me down into the pits of fear, condemnation, and control. I had completely forgotten the freedom that I had once enjoyed. I was now wrapped in a different kind of chain, one that looked good outwardly but was filled with dead men's bones. When someone gets overcome with the darkness of man-made religion, they can forget what the beautiful light of his grace looks like. But there was a light coming and God was planning a jail break.

8

THE GOSPEL JAILBREAK

L IKE SLAVES OFTEN do we had settled into our misery and just figured that this was what it meant to be "sold out" to Jesus. We comforted each other with words of pride and flattery, saying that we were the elite of the Christian faith. That's why we gave up so much and spent our lives in a state of personal self-sacrifice. To be honest with you, if that's what I thought I had to do to serve Jesus correctly, I would still be there today. I owe him my life. Before he set me free I had no life, but the man-made bondage I was experiencing was not his plan for my life at all.

Despite my environment, the passion of my life and my distaste for condemnation was something God had placed deep within me. Through a series of events I had some friends approach me and tell me about a man that hated condemnation as much as I did. I was curious and I checked this guy out. Well, when I turned to his teachings it was like taking a fresh breath of air after holding your breath for ten years. This guy was preaching the gospel; he was shining the light on man-made religion's darkness and bringing Jesus back to the church.

My wife and I were absolutely exhilarated. We sat and listened to the preaching of the gospel like starving little children. We were once again feeding on Jesus. We were once again enjoying the bread of life. We were being reminded of the simplicity of Christ.

That mighty gospel was shining the light of its glorious freedom into our prison cell of man-made religion and chains were popping off daily. We were being restored to the joy of our salvation. We were falling back in love with Jesus. Our tired, weary hands were breaking under the yoke of man-pleasing and Jesus was inviting us to come under the yoke of his eternal love, the yoke of his amazing grace. These were exciting days for us. We were once again excited about God. Furthermore, we immediately began to see fruit in our lives.

This caused no small stir; freedom and control cannot occupy the same place. We had to eventually shake the dust off of our feet and move on with our lives. We were grateful for all that we had learned at the old church, but we had rediscovered the pearl of great price. We had rediscovered Jesus. We had rediscovered grace. Freedom flooded our lives once again and we were brought back to the place where we had first started. We were brought back to HIS amazing grace.

I don't want to the give the sense that we just floated out into happily ever after once we began to hear the gospel again. We definitely had challenges. It was difficult to restore our minds to freedom after we had spent so much time in religious slavery. We are *still* learning. One of the challenging things about freedom is that it brings an opportunity to mature.

There is no maturity in slavery; you just do what your told. You don't have to think for yourself or really have any relationship with God of your own. Someone else hears God for you and then you do what they tell you to do as if God told you to do it. Freedom allows us to mature and have a relationship with God for ourselves. Without the freedom of amazing grace, we will never venture out into the spirit-led life. So there were definitely growing pains as we embraced this freedom, but the discomfort of being forced to grow up was easily worth the cost of being set free.

9

JESUS CAME TO
BRING FREEDOM

JESUS IS YOUR champion. He broke down the prison walls and he swung open the cell-block doors of man's misery. He is standing, smiling, with the keys in his hands, calling our names. He wants to set us free from sin and fear and shame and you name it—he has come to set us free from it. Jesus is your champion. He is your liberator. He is your savior. Your mighty king does not want anything to have control over you. He is your king and his kingdom runs on love and liberty.

God always had freedom on his mind; he created us. In the garden we lost that freedom. Jesus came to bring that freedom back. Jesus came to set the captives free. He came to open prison doors. Jesus is a liberator, not a dictator. Galatians 5:1 says, "It is for freedom that Christ has set us free. Stand firm, then, and do not let yourselves be burdened again by a yoke of slavery."

It is *for* freedom that you have been set free. You have been set free for the purpose of *enjoying* the freedom that only Jesus can provide. Your freedom was, is, and always will be important to Jesus. He was willing to die for it and he encourages us to not go back to a yoke of slavery.

God is *not* interested in controlling you. He is *not* interested in enslaving you. He didn't create you to be a slave; he created you to be a son, he created you to be a daughter. Your future is bright in him. Jesus has come to bring you the freedom that only heaven can provide.

When most people think of Christianity, I don't think the word *freedom* is the first word that pops into their minds. In fact, it's probably the opposite. I spent the first 19 years of my life as an atheist. I was pretty outspoken against Christianity and when I looked at the Christians around me the word *freedom* would probably be the last word I would use to describe them. I would have probably used words like *boring*, *weak minded*, and *controlled*.

As a teenager I would look at the Christians and think, "Man, you guys aren't having any fun at all." Christianity did not look like freedom to me. In fact, it just looked like more rules, more lists of things I couldn't do. Yet scriptures clearly say Jesus came to bring freedom. In fact, the Bible says this in 2 Corinthians 3:17: "Now the Lord is the Spirit; and where the Spirit of the Lord is, there is freedom."

Wherever God's presence is, in that place, there will be freedom. Man-made religion runs on fear and control. God's kingdom runs on love and liberty. If God's spirit is in a place, there will be freedom there. Just because there is a steeple and a church building does not mean God's spirit is there. Now, I know God is omnipresent. Yes, as our creator, he truly is everywhere, but, his *manifest* presence is not everywhere.

10

MAN–MADE RELI– GION'S SLAVERY

MY SON PLAYS soccer, so I spend a good portion of my time around soccer fields. I can remember one Saturday when I was waiting on one of his games to start, I strolled down to another field to check out a game that was going on to pass the time. What I saw broke my heart. There was a little girl probably about eight or nine years old playing in a game. Her father was on the sidelines yelling at her constantly. Nothing she did was right or good enough. The dad just angrily barked constant demands of her. "You are not moving fast enough." "You need to make better passes." "You need to try harder." "What's wrong with you?" The little girl looked completely miserable. My heart ached for her. She couldn't do anything to please her father. She wasn't enjoying the game and I'm sure she wasn't enjoying her relationship with her father either.

Have you ever had a relationship with someone and you could never measure up to their standard? You were always trying to get them to love you or to like you. Ultimately, I'm sure it was not a relationship you really enjoyed. You probably never felt like you could be yourself, probably always felt like you were pretending or being fake, because that person probably made you feel that who you really were was simply not good enough for them.

In a relationship like this there is no real freedom. You are always trying to live up to someone else's expectations and always feeling like you don't measure up. That is not freedom; that is bondage. One of the greatest of all freedoms is being loved. One of the greatest of all bondages is trying to earn love.

Love and approval are two awesome and powerful things. All of creation hungers to be loved and approved. All creation hungers for love because all of creation came from love. The Bible says that God is love. Love created everything. So deep inside all of creation is the desire to be loved. The Bible makes it very clear in John 3:16–17: "For God so loved the world that he gave his only begotten son, that whoever believes in him should not perish but have everlasting life. For God did not send his son into the world to condemn the world, but that the world through him might be saved."

God loves the whole world and he demonstrated that love by sending Jesus to die for our sins. Sometimes I think the way some people present Christianity is that God loves only Christians. That's not what that verse says; it says God loves the *whole* world.

Man-made religion presents a system where we try to earn God's love and approval. This is not freedom. This is the ultimate bondage. God never intended for you to earn anything from him. He prepared all of it for you to enjoy. He has freely demonstrated the all-consuming depths of his love for you with the cross.

God doesn't want you to try and earn his love. He just wants you to receive it and enjoy it. The greatest thing you can do for God is just believe and receive his love for you. He loves you *so* much and he wants you to enjoy his love. Love always brings freedom, because love drives out fear. Fear always brings bondage, because it always facilitates torment. First John 4:18 says, "There is no fear in love; but perfect love drives out fear, because fear involves torment. But he who fears has not been made perfect in love."

God wants his love to set you so free that you

become perfect in love. The word for "perfect" in the Greek is *teleioō*; it means to bring to an end, to complete, to perfect.

God wants to make you complete in his love. His love will make you whole. It will make you healthy. It will make you free. His love will do a work in your heart that is so powerful that it will make you fearless. You will no longer hunger and thirst for the approval of man, but you will walk free from its snare. Proverbs 29:25 says: "The fear of man brings a snare, but whoever trusts in the LORD shall be safe."

Man-made religion runs on snares. It creates an environment based in bondage. With whip cracks from angry taskmasters, congregations are subdued and enslaved in an unhealthy fear of man. God never called you to fear a man, or any human being for that matter. Fear motivated by religious obligation tears down the people of God like a car running on the wrong kind of fuel. A car running on fuel that it wasn't designed to run on, over a period of time, starts to break down and perform worse and worse.

That's why people get burned out on going to church. Most ministries are running on the engines of guilt, fear, and obligation. Human beings don't function well driven by guilt, and over time it begins to tear them down and destroy them. The new covenant that

Jesus provides is not driven by guilt, fear, and obligation. The new covenant is love driven. Human beings function well when they are loved, and love motivates them to action, not guilt and fear. You are at your very best when you are being loved and loving. *This* is what church is supposed to be about. His love brings true freedom.

When you walk into a room and flip the light switch on, you don't see a struggle as darkness tries to fight back against the light. In the presence of light darkness is instantly absent. The light drives out the darkness so fast you can't even see it. Love does the same thing with fear. The eviction notice is so swift that fear becomes an immediate memory in the presence of love.

Love brings freedom. That's why there is such a contrast between man-made religion and the love of God. Religion is fear driven and always sucks all the liberty right out of the room.

Right now, I just want to invite you to stop here and pray with me. Many of us have been terribly hurt by man-made religion. There is very powerful and important healing that God wants to bring into these wounds. The first thing you have to realize—and this may seem a little strange and off topic—but you are completely forgiven. Embrace the power of that forgiveness; let the strength of his amazing grace wash over your mind.

You are eternally forgiven, because of the finished work of the cross. You may be asking, "Why is it so important for me to realize that, Jeremiah? What does my forgiveness have to do with receiving healing from the wounds in my heart?" It's because you cannot give what you haven't first received. The power of the reality of God's forgiveness needs to come to you and roll through you, like a tidal wave.

In order for healing to truly happen you have to forgive those people that hurt you. They are not the enemy; the devil is the enemy. Your battle is not with them, they were used by the enemy to hurt you and now it's time to take the power of his amazing grace and apply it to this situation. It's time for you to be set free, by forgiving those that were used by the enemy to hurt you. Pray this with me:

God, I receive your forgiveness for me. I am completely and totally forgiven from now into the depths of eternity because of the blood of Jesus. Now, I choose to let that forgiveness roll through me and set me free from the chains that are trying to hold me. I forgive _____ [put in the names of those who have hurt you];

the same powerful forgiveness that you have given me, I give it to them.

Now, pray for them and pray that God will bless them and set them free from what has been hurting them and those around them.

You, my friend, are moving forward, moving into the health and freedom that Jesus has provided for you. For many of you this will be a moment when many chains break off of your life forever. We love you and we believe in you. Your greatest days are ahead of you.

11

THE LAW OF LIBERTY

ONE OF THE things that God has given us to ensure our freedom is the law of liberty. It may sound almost like an oxymoron. How can a law bring liberty? Constraint and freedom sound like they are on opposite ends of the spectrum. How can you be constrained and liberated at the same time? Many times when we think of the word *law* we think in terms of "don't do this" and" don't do that," but there is much more to the meaning of this word.

In the Greek it's the word *nomo*. It can certainly mean "law" in the traditional sense but it can also mean a principal or force compelling us. Perhaps bringing it forth in a way we are more familiar with will help us to understand. I'm sure you have heard of the law of gravity. Gravity is a constant force that is exerted on earth. It's not used in the sense of it being a rule or a standard that can be kept or disregarded, but instead it's a force and a principal to help us understand the way things operate.

When God speaks of the law of liberty he is talking about the force behind our freedom. There are so many things constantly trying to bring us back into bondage that Father God has lovingly given us a force to protect our freedom. It's one thing to be set free; it's another thing to stay free. In order for us to stay free we have to have a force that is greater than the forces that are trying to bring us back into bondage.

We have looked at many different forms of bondage, from worldly bondage to man-made religious bondage. This world is filled with things that will try to steal our freedom but God has a plan to set us free and keep us free.

God's ultimate plan for us has always been freedom and with so many prison pitfalls of bondage, on this earth in order to stay free we have to access this law of liberty.

Now we know that Jesus is our liberator, and as our liberator he has brought in a new covenant that has a completely different dynamic than the old one. God gave us this force of freedom to keep us free from anything that would try to bring us back into bondage.

Let's take a look at this law of liberty in scripture.

James 1:25 says: "But he who looks into the perfect law of liberty and continues in it, and is not a forgetful hearer but a doer of the work, this one will be blessed in what he does."

Immediately we see that this law of liberty is designed to bring blessing into our lives; it's going to bring blessing in what we do. Let's take a look at the word *blessing* so we are all on the same page about what it means. In the Greek the word for "blessing" is the word *makarios*. *Makarios* is defined: ("blessed") describes a believer in enviable ("fortunate") position from receiving God's provisions (favor)—His grace (benefits) fortunate, well off:—blessed, happy.

Judging from the definition of this beautiful Greek word, this is something I think we all want in our lives. This law of liberty brings this state of blessing into our lives. God always has a plan for our good. There is a certain beautiful freedom in simply being happy, which is a big part of the meaning of this word.

Let's take a look at what would cause us not to operate in this law of liberty. The warning in this passage of scripture is not to forget: "not a forgetful hearer but a doer of the work." So if the scripture is warning us not to forget and forgetting has the ability to hamper this blessing in our lives, then it must be something that can happen easily and we need to guard against it. The question is, "To forget what?" We will get to that in a moment but let's look at this scripture in its context first to help us understand what is being said.

James 1:22–25 says: "But be doers of the word, and not hearers only, deceiving yourselves. For if anyone is a hearer of the word and not a doer, he is like a man observing his natural face in a mirror; for he observes himself, goes away, and immediately forgets what kind of man he was. But he who looks into the perfect law of liberty and continues in it, and is not a forgetful hearer but a doer of the work, this one will be blessed in what he does."

This passage of scripture has been greatly misunderstood in the past. What God intended to bring freedom, many times man has used to do the exact opposite, bring bondage. People have used this passage of scripture to condemn and control people rather than setting them free. Let's begin to break this passage down line by line.

James 1:21 says: "Be doers of the word and not hearers only, deceiving yourselves."

People often use this passage of scripture to say, "Yep, you need to be a doer of the word! That's your problem: you're not a doer, you're just a hearer!" When people preach from that perspective they are basically inviting us to operate on our own will power rather than God's grace.

This is the way I had always heard it taught in the past. "You just need to try harder and *do* the word more!" Truly, salvation is more about submission than conquest. A drowning man can't save himself, but he can consent to being saved. We wouldn't go to a drowning man and say, "You just need to swim more! What's wrong with you? You just need to try harder!"

A drowning man doesn't need good advice; a drowning man needs to be saved. He needs a savior to rescue him from the waters that are destroying and consuming him. Commanding people to "do the word" doesn't mean they are going to be able to do it any more than a drowning man can be forced to swim through a command.

Christianity cannot be performed through the strength of our willpower; it was never designed to be. When people teach this passage of scripture from that perspective, they are basically setting people up to fail.

What this passage of scripture is actually introducing is a tremendous force to set us free and to keep us free. Let's move on to verse 23: "For if anyone is a hearer of the word and not a doer, he is like a natural man observing his face in the mirror."

We see the problem is a breakdown between what they are hearing and what they are doing. I would like to insert here that nobody on earth is always perfect in their behavior all the time. One of the things that must be overcome in the body of Christ is this facade of always being perfect. First of all, it's a lie, and second of all it puts unnecessary pressure on people's lives.

I'm *not* saying we should live in a sloppy, loose manner that brings reproach against the gospel of grace, but I am just saying that we should hold ourselves to a loving standard of grace, not a rigid, legalistic, standard of performance. We all have plenty of times when our hearing of the word does not line up with our doing of the word. Yes, we want to live changed lives that glorify God and line up with our new nature, but this will not happen through "trying harder" or the pressure to be perfect. We need to develop more cultures of grace, not more cultures of performance.

That being said, let's get back to looking at the problem this passage is addressing. Someone is hearing, but what they're hearing is not producing and maintaining a change in their doing or their behavior.

Verse 24 goes on to say, "For he observes himself,

goes away, and immediately forgets what kind of man he was."

So this is the individual that is looking in the mirror: they see themselves clearly, they go away from the mirror, and they forget what kind of person they are. They forget! All of a sudden we see the real issue. The reason what they're doing is not lining up with their hearing is that they have forgotten who they are! Now, at this point you might say, "Really, Jeremiah, who forgets who they are?" I'm not talking about amnesia in the sense that you forget your name, who your family is, and where you live. I'm talking about a different kind of forgetting. I'm talking about forgetting that you had a change of identity when you stepped into Christ. Second Corinthians 5:17 says it like this: "Therefore, if anyone is in Christ, he is a new creation; old things have passed away; behold, all things have become new."

When we receive Jesus as our savior, our old identity dies; we become crucified with Christ and we receive a new identity in him. We become the righteousness of God in him. Our job is to renew our minds to this change of identity. We are changed on the inside but now we must put on this new man in terms of renewing our mind to this reality. Ephesians 4:22–24 says it like this: "that you put off, concerning your former conduct, the old man which grows corrupt according to the deceitful lusts, and be renewed in the spirit of your mind, and that you put on the new man which was created according to God, in true righteousness and holiness."

Jesus did all the work in giving us a new nature; our part is to renew our minds by believing what he says about us more than what anyone else has said and even more than what we think and say about ourselves. This what Romans 12:2 means when it says: "And do not be conformed to this world, but be transformed by the renewing of your mind, that you may prove what is that good and acceptable and perfect will of God."

A caterpillar already has a butterfly in its DNA, but it doesn't actually transform until there is a cocoon. God wants to surround you with a cocoon of his love so you will be transformed into the person that he already knows is within you. This law of liberty is a cocoon of transformation that will set you free and keep you free from being bound by the person you used to be. A strong, lasting freedom will only be the fruit of your new identity, not your willpower.

12

FREEDOM IN ACTION

L ET ME SHARE a story about my life that may help to illustrate this and make it more clear. When I first got saved, I really struggled with drugs and drug addiction. (I've already shared some of my experience in the first part of this book.) My deliverance was a slow process. I just don't have one of those testimonies where I got delivered from everything all at once. No, the chains of addiction popped off my life slowly. I got set free from the harder stuff first—crack, cocaine, crystal meth, pills, LSD, etc.—but the final stronghold of drug addiction in my life was marijuana.

I really struggled with marijuana for quite some time after I was saved. I had finally gotten to a place where I hadn't smoked pot in a couple of years. At that time I had been doing some running for exercise and we had this huge hill by our house that I had been using to train on for a couple of months. One day I was running up the hill and I just happened to glance down as I was running and I saw a joint. (That's a marijuana cigarette for you holy, holy, holy folks that might not know... *just kidding!*)

I saw it, and it stopped me in my tracks. Immediately temptation came rushing in on me like a tidal wave. The devil is the tempter and he never stops trying to destroy our lives through any avenue he can try to find an entrance. In that short moment when I glanced down at that joint my mind was flooded with the memories of the good times. (He never includes all the horrible devastating memories, just the good ones.) Thoughts of "No one will know" and "Hey, it's not that big of a deal," etc. ran through my mind. All of these things that I'm describing happened in just a flashing moment.

I used to spend all of my money on this, steal from my family and friends to get it; it used to be the number one priority in my life. Just out of curiosity, I leaned over and picked it up to smell it, just to make sure it really was marijuana and not tobacco. I smelled it and sure enough it was marijuana—and not just any marijuana, it was the funky stuff. (For those of you that might not know that means it was strong marijuana.)

This stuff used to rule my life, and the enemy was

trying to bring me back into a place of bondage, but do you know what I did? I dropped that thing back down onto the pavement and ground it into to the asphalt and kept running. As I continued to run, these words came out of my mouth: "I am not a pothead!" Was I tempted? Yes. Had the enemy set up a trap to ensnare me? Yes. But the power of realizing my identity was stronger than the lie the enemy was trying to get me to believe. With this temptation the enemy was trying to get me to forget who I was. He was trying to convince me that I was someone that was still addicted.

I stopped being a drug addict the moment I got saved. I became a new creation in Christ Jesus as soon as I believed; now, it took my behavior some time to catch up with what had already happened in my heart. It was just a matter of me renewing my mind to my new identity in Jesus. I was now in Christ and the old me had passed away; now I had become a new man in Christ.

This is the law of liberty, the freedom to be who God created you to be rather than believing a lie about who you are. The realization of my identity kept me free from going back to those old behaviors. The law of liberty kept me free.

Now, let me ask you a question: if I smoked the joint that day, would it have made me a pothead? Some would stop here and say, yes, if you smoked that marijuana that day you would be a "pothead." This is where the rubber meets the road in our understanding of the law of liberty. Did that action have the ability to change my nature? Would that action be so strong and so powerful that it would have the ability to undo the work of the cross within me? Would I stop being a child of God because of my mistake?

No, I don't believe that mistake would be more powerful than the cross. If I get my hands dirty, the dirt does not have the power to change the nature of my hands. The dirt remains separate from my hands even though my hands may be covered in dirt. The dirt doesn't have the power to become one with my hands. No, I just wash my hands and the dirt comes off. My hands never changed at all; they just got dirty.

The finished work of the cross is so powerful that sin doesn't have the ability to touch your born-again spirit. When you receive Jesus as your Lord and savior you become the righteousness of God in him. No one can take that away from you, not even you. The cross was way too powerful for that. The blood of Jesus is too pure! The hand of God is too strong! It was an eternal, powerful work that was wrought by the hand of God. The hands of men are just not powerful enough to undo the cross. Jesus really did finish the work on the cross; our part is to simply believe.

Well, let's take it a step further: let's say not only did I smoke that joint that day, but I continued to smoke marijuana after that. Let's say that I continued to smoke it every day for six months. Now, things are getting a little trickier. I ask you the same question: am I now a drug addict again? I may look like a drug addict, I may talk like a drug addict, I may live like a drug addict, but if I understand the power of the cross, the reality is that *I am not* a drug addict. I am a child of God who has simply lost his way. I looked into the mirror of my identity and forgot who I was. Let's look at another scripture real quick, Colossians 3:9–10: "Do not lie to one another, since you have put off the old man with his deeds, and have put on the new man who is renewed in knowledge according to the image of Him who created him."

It says, "Do not lie to one another since you have put off the old man with his deeds." Now, certainly this refers to literally lying but it means so much more than that. The lying that's being referred to here is primarily dealing with someone lying against their identity.

When we go back to old behavior we are putting on a mask and acting like something we're not. If I went back to drug addiction it wouldn't change who I was in Jesus but I would be wearing a mask that was a lie. If I could just get back to the perfect law of liberty, I could once again look into the mirror of his grace and be reminded who I am. Then the mask would simply fall off and I would remain free from the bondage of drug addiction through the power of identity and not will-power. The challenge is when people walk away from that mirror, forget who they are, go back to old behavior, and then believe that mask has become who they are.

The devil is always trying to attack your identity and get you to believe a false image about yourself. When we believe a false image about ourselves we cannot enjoy freedom. We will live under the bondage of the lying mask and embrace a false image. It is then that we become hearers of the word and not doers because we have forgotten who we are. All we need to do is hear the gospel again and be reminded of who we were in Christ.

Second Corinthians 4:3–4 says, "But even if our gospel is veiled, it is veiled to those who are perishing, whose minds the god of this age has blinded, who do not believe, lest the light of the gospel of the glory of Christ, who is the image of God, should shine on them."

The gospel shines Jesus into the hearts of the lost and gives them hope for salvation, an invitation to be saved. The gospel also shines Jesus into the hearts of the saved and reminds us who we are. Second Corinthians 3:18 says: "But we all, with unveiled face, beholding as in a mirror the glory of the Lord, are being transformed into the same image from glory to glory, just as by the Spirit of the Lord."

When we look into a normal mirror it shines back our own reflection; when we gaze into this mirror of the glory of the Lord it shines Jesus and transforms us into that same image from glory to glory. It's supernatural! It's amazing and it's the plan of God to set us free from the chains of old un-Christlike behavior. Not a lot of self-effort is needed here, just a decision to behold Jesus in all of his beauty and glory. Now that we have stepped into Christ, he has become our identity. Galatians 3:26–28 says: "For you are all sons of God through faith in Christ Jesus. For as many of you as were baptized into Christ have put on Christ. There is neither Jew nor Greek, there is neither slave nor free, there is neither male nor female; for you are all one in Christ Jesus."

When we stepped into Christ through faith in him, he became our identity; our old identity passed away. He is the head and we are his body. First John goes on to say: "Love has been perfected among us in this: that we may have boldness in the day of judgment; because as he is, so are we in this world."

We have been made one with Christ and he has become our true identity, but sometimes we need to be reminded; this is the law of liberty in action. We don't look into the scriptures primarily to see what's wrong with us; we look into the Bible to see Jesus and be transformed into the same image from glory to glory. If we look at the preceding passage, it begins in 2 Corinthians 3:17 with "Now the Lord is the Spirit; and where the Spirit of the Lord is, there is liberty. But we all, with unveiled face, beholding as in a mirror the glory of the Lord, are being transformed into the same image from glory to glory, just as by the Spirit of the Lord."

The ultimate freedom is discovering who you are and living in that identity. Perhaps the greatest bondage is to believe that you are something or someone that you are not. One of the greatest things we suffer from in the body of Christ and in the whole world is identity crisis. For example, how could I ever be free from the behavior of a drug addict if I still believed that I was one? We are going to behave according to who we believe that we are. When Jesus changed my identity, I needed to begin to relate to this new creation that he had made me rather than identifying with the old. If I still actively believe that I am something I am not, then how am I ever going to change? Let's get back to the mirror in the law of liberty in James 1:23–25: "For if anyone is a hearer of the word and not a doer, he is like a man observing his natural face in a mirror; for he observes himself, goes away, and immediately forgets what kind of man he was. But he who looks into the perfect law of liberty and continues in it, and is not a forgetful hearer but a doer of the work, this one will be blessed in what he does."

So how do we continue in the law of liberty and be doers of the word and not hearers only? How do we cause or behavior to line up with our identity and live lives of freedom and not bondage? *We keep beholding Jesus* and we embrace him as our new identity. Then we won't forget who we are and go back to our old ways.

We may have moments of weakness and forgetfulness and go back to dumb stuff but we just need to be reminded again and not let the devil convince us that we are those mistakes we make. Just like when the temptation came in for me to drugs again: I said, "*I am not a drug addict.*" This brings us to the next element of the law of liberty. Let's look again at James 1:22–26: "But be doers of the word, and not hearers only, deceiving yourselves. For if anyone is a hearer of the word and not a doer, he is like a man observing his natural face in a mirror; for he observes himself, goes away, and immediately forgets what kind of man he was. But he who looks into the perfect law of liberty and continues in it, and is not a forgetful hearer but a doer of the work, this one will be blessed in what he does. If anyone among you thinks he is religious, and does not bridle his tongue but deceives his own heart, this one's religion is useless."

We must speak in line with our new nature if we expect to really live in its reality. If I said when that temptation faced me, "I'm just a drug addict and I will always be a drug addict," it would be a real challenge for me not to act that out. Our words are powerful and our tongue is the rudder of our life. Our actions will ultimately line up with our words. James 3:3–5 says: "Indeed, we put bits in horses' mouths that they may obey us, and we turn their whole body. Look also at ships: although they are so large and are driven by fierce winds, they are turned by a very small rudder wherever the pilot desires. Even so the tongue is a little member and boasts great things."

Our tongue controls the direction of our lives. If we want to manifest the reality of our identity we absolutely must speak in line with who God has made us to be. If I continued to say out of my mouth these last 17 years that "I am a drug addict," you can bet that's exactly what would show up in my behavior. At some point we have to begin to speak in line with our identity if we want to access the law of liberty and swing free from the bondages of the past.

God changes our nature but he wants us to renew our minds and speak in agreement with what he already knows about us. There has been a lot of teaching on this in the body of Christ already but it bears repeating. There is tremendous power in what we say. If you think about it, it's how we got saved in the first place. We believed in our hearts and we spoke out of our mouths. Proverbs 18:21 it says, "Death and life are in the power of the tongue, And those who love it will eat its fruit."

When we begin to tap into the law of liberty and see ourselves as we truly are and then speak in line with this new nature, we begin to enjoy the fruit of this amazing new identity Jesus has given us. As I begin to see myself the way God sees me and I begin to say what God says about me, the fruit of the spirit begins to manifest in my life. I'm sure you are familiar with the fruit of the spirit, but let's look at this verse real quick in Galatians 5:22–23: "the fruit of the Spirit is love, joy, peace, longsuffering, kindness, goodness, faithfulness, gentleness, self-control. Against such there is no law."

These amazing fruits that come from our born-again spirit bring a freedom in our lives that everyone can see. Jesus drops the shackles when we receive him as savior but these fruits display the freedom outwardly that we already have on the inside. The challenge is that people have tried to produce these fruits by gritting their teeth and straining their will power. Lasting change will never be a result of self-directed effort but of beholding Jesus and gliding on the force of freedom that we call the law of liberty.

If you look at the next verse in that passage of scripture, it says in verse 24: "And those who are Christ's have crucified the flesh with its passions and desires."

Folks try so hard to crucify the flesh that they live their lives trying to accomplish what Jesus has already accomplished on the cross. Galatians 2:20 says: "I have been crucified with Christ; it is no longer I who live, but Christ lives in me."

So if we have already, past tense, been crucified with Christ, why is he encouraging us to crucify the flesh? Once again it goes back to the law of liberty and the power of our words. Remember James 1:25–26: "But he who looks into the perfect law of liberty and continues in it, and is not a forgetful hearer but a doer of the work, this one will be blessed in what he does. If anyone among you thinks he is religious, and does not bridle his tongue but deceives his own heart, this one's religion is useless."

If we continue to speak and agree with our old nature, it renders the law of liberty powerless to keep us free. Our freedom is dependent upon our agreeing with our new identity and speaking in line with it. This is crucifying the flesh and reminding ourselves that we are not the person we used to be. Without our words lining up with our new identity, it will be easy to walk away from the mirror and forget who we are. But if we continue in the law of liberty and bridle our tongue with its reality we won't deceive our own heart and we will manifest the fruit of the spirit that is already within us and we will fulfill the scripture in Galatians 5:22–25: "But the fruit of the Spirit is love, joy, peace, longsuffering, kindness, goodness, faithfulness, gentleness, self- control. Against such there is no law. And those who are Christ's have crucified the flesh with its passions and desires. If we live in the Spirit, let us also walk in the Spirit."

We will walk in the spirit, manifesting the fruit of the spirit and live in the freedom of our new identity.

I gained a new identity when I received Jesus; when I act contrary to that new identity and go back to the old behavior of the person I used to be, I am lying against the truth. I am acting like something I'm not. If I kept using the drugs I would by lying against the truth, but the truth within me would be more powerful than the mistakes around me. I just needed to be reminded who I was by the power of the amazing good news of the gospel and let that law of freedom keep me free.

13

FREEDOM USED AGAINST US

TRULY THE DEVIL hates our freedom and he wants to stop it any way he can. I think he hates it so much because he lost so much of his when he fell. As we begin to get set free from man-made religions bondage, we enter into the wide-open fields of amazing grace. It takes time to get accustomed to freedom, and it takes time to get our bearings and learn how to truly function in freedom. This is especially true when so many of us have spent our lives living in some form of slavery.

When we begin to walk in freedom, often we are not really sure how to act. I have found that many people begin by testing the boundaries. Is this love really unconditional? Is this love really never-ending? Is there really nothing I can do stop God from loving me? In man-made religion we were used to being quickly rejected when we made a mistake and almost like orphaned, abused children, we want to make sure that this love is for real. So the exploring begins as we walk through these fields of freedom and amazing grace. Father God is lovingly smiling, watching over us as we move forward.

Peter made this statement about Paul's message in 2 Peter 3:15–16: "our beloved brother Paul, according to the wisdom given to him, has written to you, as also in all his epistles, speaking in them of these things, in which are some things hard to understand, which untaught and unstable people twist to their own destruction, as they do also the rest of the scriptures."

Peter says some folks are misunderstanding what Paul is saying and it is being twisted unto their own destruction. What is he talking about here? Paul came preaching a message of freedom from the law and an invitation to embrace the grace of God. This was intended to bring an amazing freedom into people's lives, but freedom can be dangerous in the sense that people will have opportunity to abuse it. However, just because people abuse freedom doesn't mean we should stop setting people free.

God is not afraid of our freedom. Scripture (Galatians 5:1) declares, "It is for freedom that Christ has set us free." Will some people abuse this freedom?

Absolutely. Even so, unless people are set free they will never actually learn how to operate in this freedom and steward it properly.

It is like parenting: as we raise our children we want to give them greater and greater degrees of freedom to give them an opportunity to grow up. As I write this book, my son is ten years old. What if I had him under the same boundaries and rules for the rest of his life?

A 17-year-old needs different boundaries than a 5-year-old. If not, the child will never grow up and know how to handle freedom; that's why many times you see kids from very strict homes turn 18 leave the house and lose their minds in the real world. Why? They were never taught how to handle freedom and make choices for themselves. My job as a parent is to steadily increase my son's freedom as he grows up so he will know how to handle freedom when he becomes an adult.

If the enemy can't keep us from freedom, he will try to use our freedom against us. You may be saying, "Jeremiah, how could he be using something as beautiful as freedom against us?" The devil is defeated, but he is sneaky. The Bible encourages us not to be ignorant of his devices. In Galatians 5:13 we see a warning concerning our freedom: "For you, brethren, have been called to liberty; only do not use liberty as an opportunity for the flesh, but through love serve one another."

In this passage of scripture we see a warning that freedom can be used as an opportunity for the flesh. Freedom gives us options; it puts us into the driver seat of our own life, and it allows us to choose. We can choose to be spiritually minded and allow the God-given nature of love to flow through us, or we can choose to be carnally minded and allow the memories of our old fleshly behavior to guide us. Ultimately, the choice is ours, but this passage of scripture is a loving warning not to allow our freedom to be a starting point for bad decisions.

When we enter into freedom we have to be careful not to allow the enemy to destroy us with it. I have found that people that have lived their entire lifetimes restrained by fear and obligation take some time to adjust to the freedom that grace provides. People stop doing the right things for the wrong reasons and begin to allow grace to change the motives of their heart. It takes time to steward liberty with love and it doesn't happen overnight, and on the other side of it is genuine maturity. People are making right decisions for the right reasons. It is beautiful and it's something the church and the world hasn't seen too much of.

Freedom allows love to be the motivator and the

constrainer. Paul said it best in 2 Corinthians 5:13–14: "For if we are beside ourselves, it is for God; or if we are of sound mind, it is for you. For the love of Christ compels us…"

As we grow up in this freedom enjoying the grace of God, love becomes the steward over our lives. Only love can properly steward liberty. Another translation of 2 Corinthians 5:12 says it like this: "For the love of Christ constrains us…"

God's love for us compels us and constrains us, to give us a perfect balance of wisdom in the wide-open fields of amazing grace. Freedom is beautiful and it is God's will for our lives, but we can't allow the enemy to use it against us. Only love will cause us to steward our liberty with wisdom. If freedom is our ship, then love is the wind in our sails.

As the good news of the gospel begins to reveal just how much God loves you, the spirit of God will begin to cause his love to flow through you into other people's lives. This love gets so big and so strong in our lives it begins to lead us through this life. Galatians 5:13–14 says: "For you, brethren, have been called to liberty; only do not use liberty as an opportunity for the flesh, but through love serve one another. For all the law is fulfilled in one word, even in this: You shall love your neighbor as yourself."

The love of God sets the stage for us to live in freedom, but the love of God keeps us safe in this powerful freedom that has been granted to us through the cross. Only love has the power to steward this freedom. In Matthew 11:28–30 Jesus makes a very interesting statement about the difference between his yoke and the yoke of the law: "Are you tired? Worn out? Burned out on religion? Come to me. Get away with me and you'll recover your life. I'll show you how to take a real rest. Walk with me and work with me—watch how I do it. Learn the unforced rhythms of grace. I won't lay anything heavy or ill-fitting on you. Keep company with me and you'll learn to live freely and lightly."

The analogy of the yoke was a very clear picture to the agricultural-based people that he was talking to. They, of course, did not have machines and tractors like we do today. In order to plow a field for farming, they would use oxen. The big strong animals would plow the fields for them, but they would yoke the animals together in order to increase their combined strength. The yoke was a wooden piece of equipment that would bring the two oxen together so they could walk the fields in unison. They would yoke the younger oxen up to the older oxen in order to teach the younger ones how to plow the fields and what way to go.

Jesus approaches the people and declares, "I have

a different kind of yoke for you, one that is going to be easy and light. This yoke is going to lead and direct you but it is going to be different than the heavy yoke of the law that you have been used to." Jesus's yoke is a yoke of love. Jesus brings us into this place of freedom and his yoke of love warmly forms around our hearts and gently leads us in this life. First John 4:19 says: "We love because he first loved us."

He loves us first in our broken, sinful state of failure and his love lifts us up on our feet to live again. Then his love for us empowers us to love him back and love the people around us. Unlike the yoke of a legalism, Jesus's yoke provides the most amazing freedom as it guides us, because Jesus's love for us causes us to fall in love with him. His love woos us and subdues us until we are happy to let him lead us because we trust that he loves us.

It's easy to trust someone when you know without a doubt that they love you and have your best interest at heart. Jesus's love is so powerful that it drives out all doubt and gives us a confidence in his gentle loving hand. His yoke is easy and his yoke is light because we are no longer afraid. His powerful love drives out all fear and causes us to actually want to be led by him because we trust him. It is truly beautiful.

Jesus loves us first, and then his love for us

empowers us to love him back and love those around us. Jesus is the supply; he is initiator, he is the beginning, he fills us up with so much love that it begins to pour out of our lives into the lives of other people. John 7:37–38 says: "Jesus stood and cried out, saying, 'If anyone thirsts, let him come to me and drink. He who believes in me, as the scripture has said, out of his heart will flow rivers of living water.'"

God intends to fill us with so much love that liquid love begins to pour out of our hearts like rivers. I don't know if you have ever seen a strong flowing river, but it has the power to control whatever you put on it. If you put a paper boat on that river the current will carry that boat wherever the river flows. Father God intends for his love to flow so strongly to us and through us that that love begins to lead our lives in a powerful and beautiful way.

This is the yoke of Jesus. This is the law of love. This is the ultimate expression of liberty and it is the genius masterstroke of heaven to bring mankind into a heavenly harmony. Love will lead us, and love will set us free. Fear and selfishness cannot maintain their strength in the rivers of God's love. They simply shrink up and die. Man-made religion is destroyed and forgotten like sand castles in the sand as the waves of God's relentless love come crashing down on its temporary kingdom. It's hard not to wax a little poetic when talking about God's love and the freedom it brings.

Are there consequences to our actions? Absolutely! But our bad behavior will never cause God to stop loving us or reject us as his sons and daughters. He is faithful to us even when we are not faithful to him, or even ourselves. He loves us so much he doesn't want us to make decisions that will harm us or harm those around us. Freedom gives us the opportunity to mature, the opportunity to choose to do what's right because we want to know, not because we are being forced to.

Conclusion

JESUS HAS INVITED us into freedom, real freedom, not the fake freedom the world promises and not the weary manipulations of manmade religion. God began his plan with freedom and eternally punctuated that plan with the cross. There was nothing free about our freedom, which is why we should enjoy it. When we understand the cost of this freedom it will help us to understand how important it was to God that we be set free.

We don't have to fear this freedom; this is the place that genuine maturity happens. I know a lot of people fear freedom and it's usually the people who are in control. There is no place in Christianity for one group of people to control another group of people. Jesus came to set the captives free, not just direct them to another prison.

Other people fear freedom because they don't trust themselves, so they have spent much of their lives allowing other people to make all the decisions for them. I understand that; I used to be someone like that. However, you don't have to be afraid and you don't even really have to trust yourself. Trust Jesus. He will take you by the hand and lead you into this freedom. I think it's more of a journey than a destination anyway. Truth by its very nature brings freedom. Jesus said in John 8:31–32: "If you abide in My word, you are My disciples indeed. And you shall know the truth, and the truth shall make you free."

No man knows all truth. We are all learning. We are hopefully receiving more and more truth, and in turn stepping into greater degrees of freedom. This is a journey and everyone is in different place on this road. It's not time to compare yourself with somebody else. You can't rush anybody or even rush yourself. Relax and enjoy the ride.

As we have spent this time together, hopefully you have seen where it is clearly laid out in scripture that God's plan for our life is freedom. We shouldn't fear it or run from it. It is what Jesus died to provide for us and it is the only place that real maturity can actually happen.

Jesus has clearly come as a liberator, not a taskmaster.

Almighty God is on your side and his intention is to set you free and keep you free. There is an amazing adventure in front of you as we swing free from what tries to enslave us. Jesus is calling you out into his wide-open fields of amazing grace. Enjoy the journey.

In closing I want to invite you to pray a prayer with me. You may have been reading this book and some of the things I have been sharing with you have been touching your heart. My friend, if you haven't received Jesus as your Lord and Savior I invite you to do it now. The Bible says whoever calls upon the name of the Lord will be saved. God has a plan for your life and it's a plan filled with freedom and adventure. Jesus is reaching his hand out to you now, smiling and saying, "Let me set you free." If you haven't made him the Lord of your life I invite you to do it now. Pray this prayer with me out loud and from your heart:

"Jesus, I believe that you are the son of God. I believe you died on the cross for my sins. I believe that you were raised again from the dead and you are seated on the right of father God now. Jesus, I ask you to come into my life and set me free."

Welcome into the family, my friend. Please contact us and let us know how we can be a blessing to you.

In closing, I would just like to quote the words of William Wallace in all the passion and intensity with which he uttered this word:

FREEEEEEEEEEEDOOOOOOOOOOOOM!!!!!!

About Jeremiah Johnson

WITH ELEVEN YEARS of full time ministry behind him, Jeremiah is in full stride to share the good news of Jesus and his amazing grace. Jeremiah is the senior pastor at Grace Point church in Georgetown, KY. Jeremiah is also an author and has a very active traveling ministry. Jeremiah is called to bring believers into the reality of the new covenant and a deeper understanding of Jesus and his amazing grace. If you are interested in having him come and speak contact us.

Jeremiahjohnsonministries.com

gracepointgeorgetown.com

www.facebook.com/ JeremiahJohnsonMinistries

JeremiahJohnsonMinistries@ gmail.com

Twitter @Gracepoint555

42777253R00066

Made in the USA
Middletown, DE
18 April 2019